Time 2 Party!

By Sana Waseem

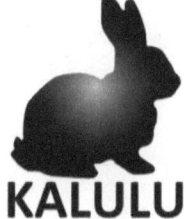

KALULU

A Publishing Company.
2019. All rights reserved.
Calgary, AB, Canada.

Dear Reader,

Thank you for purchasing this henna design book.

If you are recreating any of these designs, please make sure to reference me by using my nickname hashtag #samashenna. I love hearing from you all and seeing all your amazing work.

Enjoy!
Sana (a.k.a. Sama).

Modern

TWILIGHT

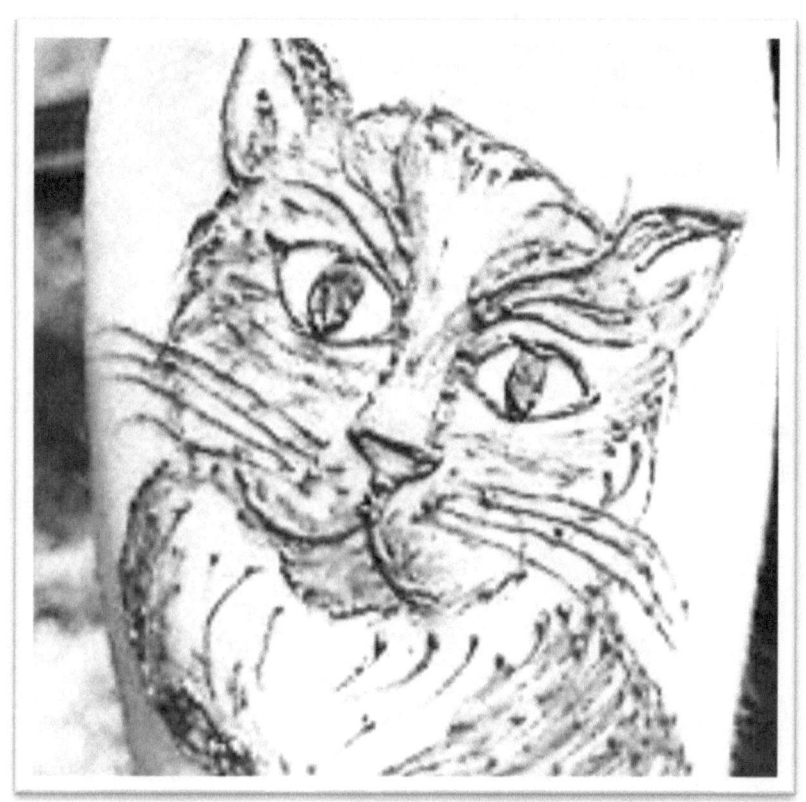

Meow

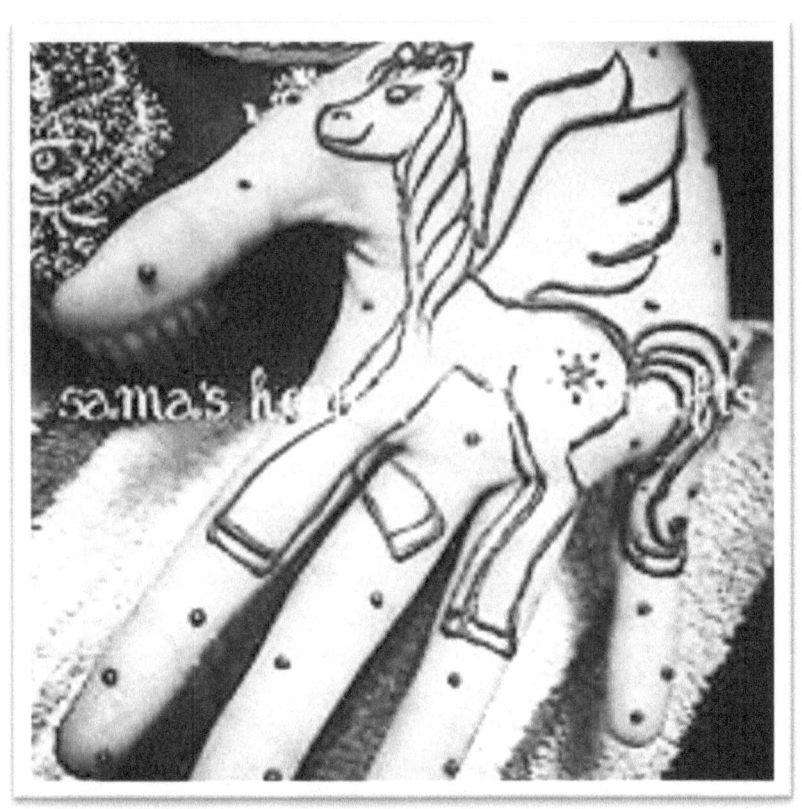

Hello Sunshine

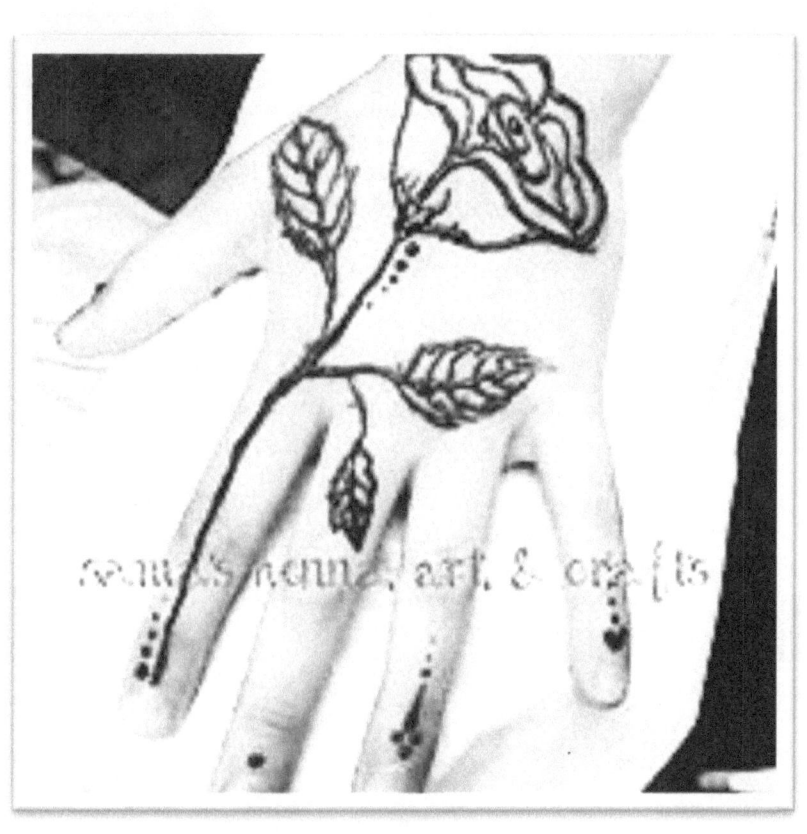

Let's get Rosy

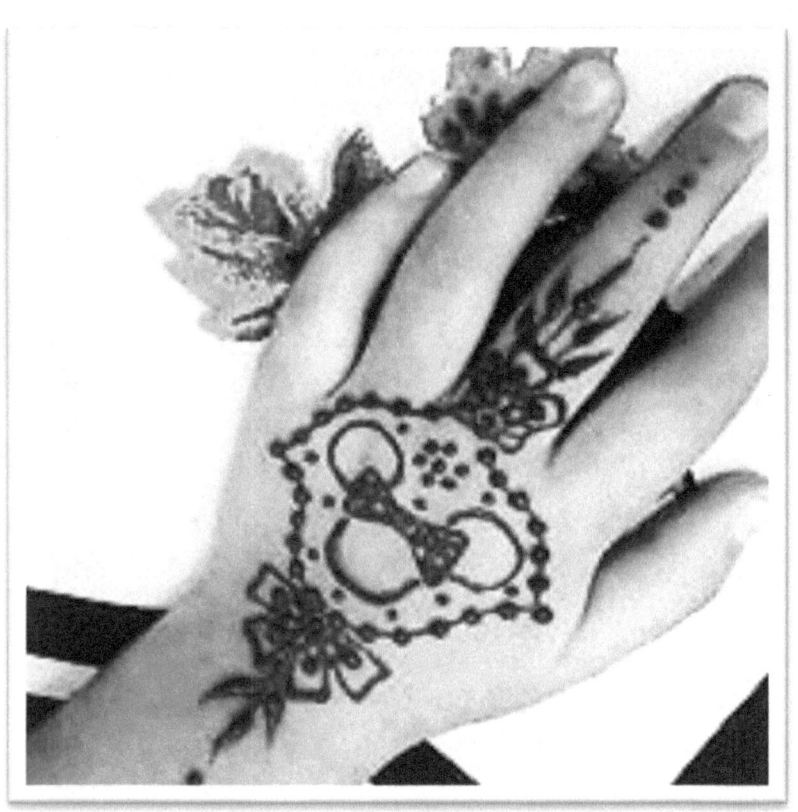

ANONyMOUSe

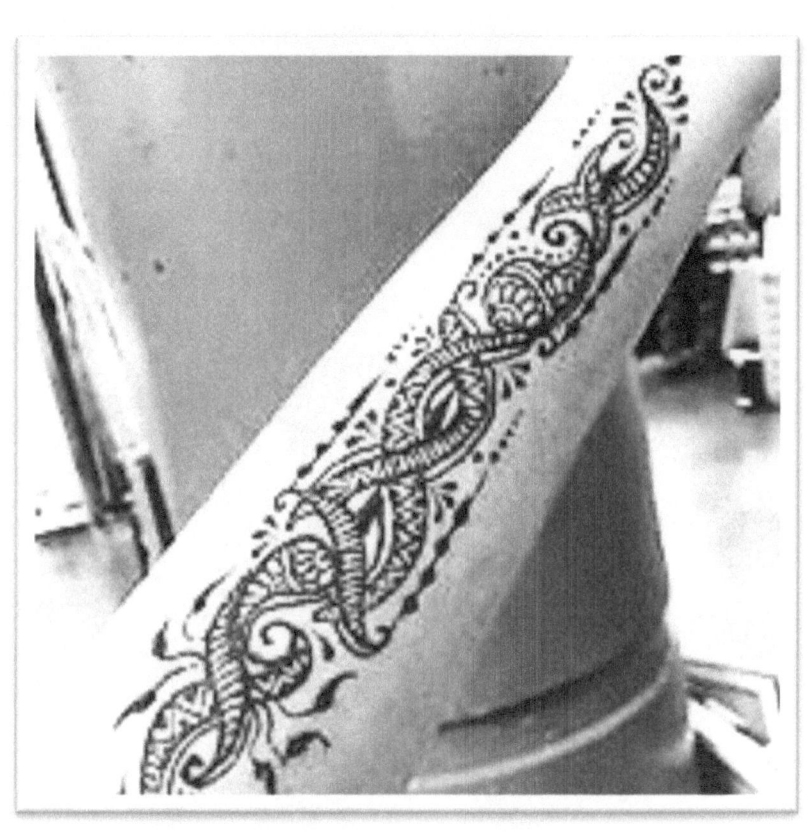

Go With the Flow

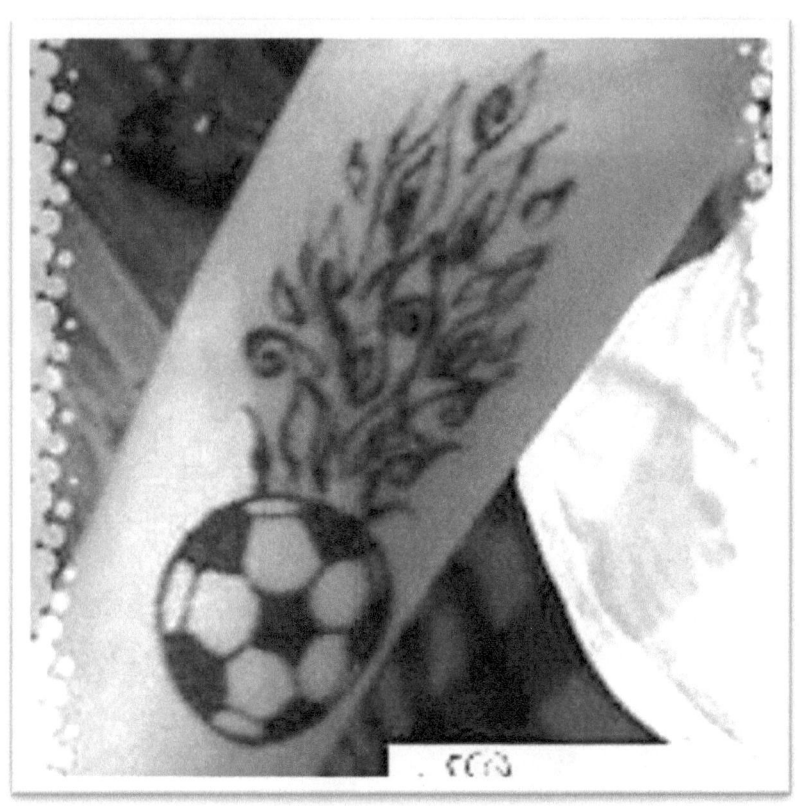

Kickin' It

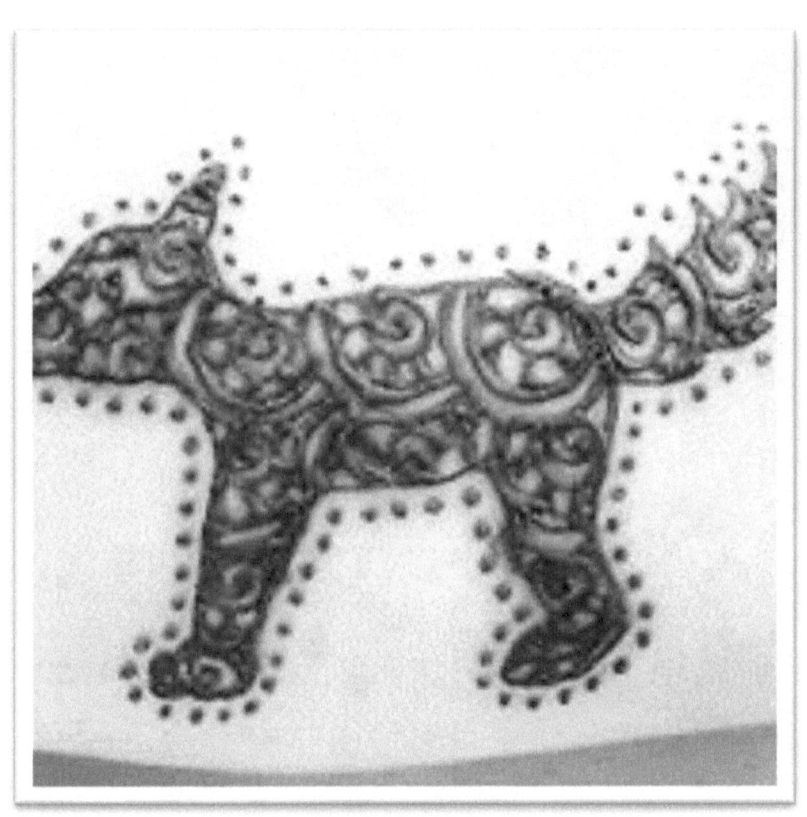

WOOF

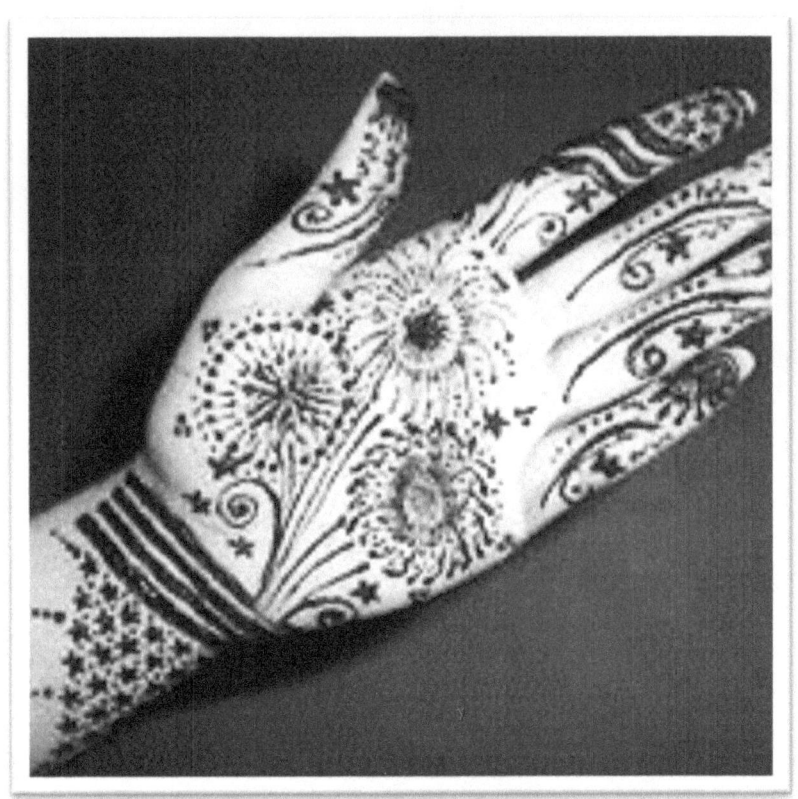

Celebrate

Traditional

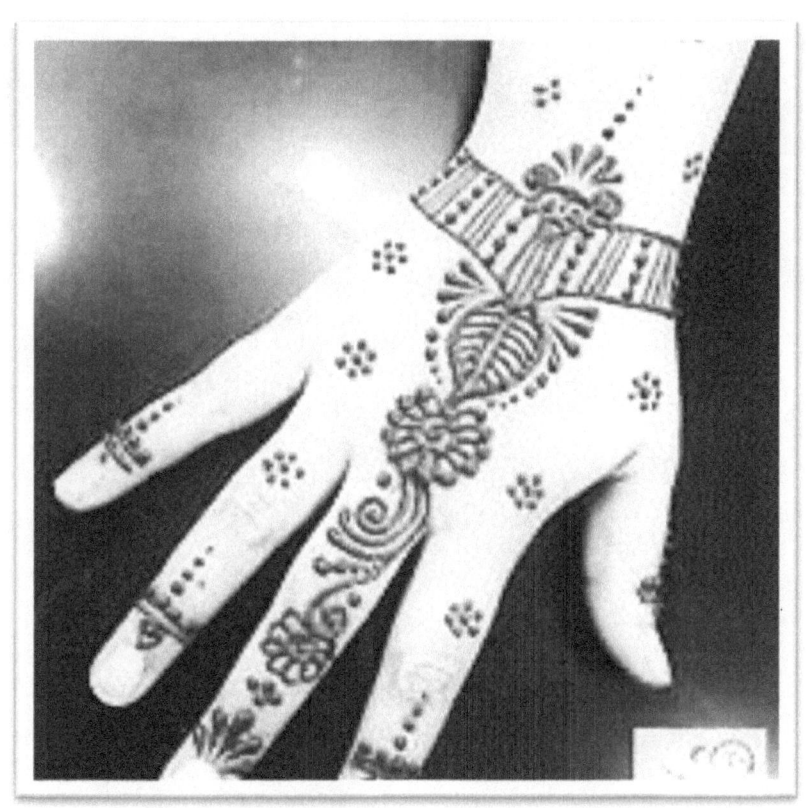

Love

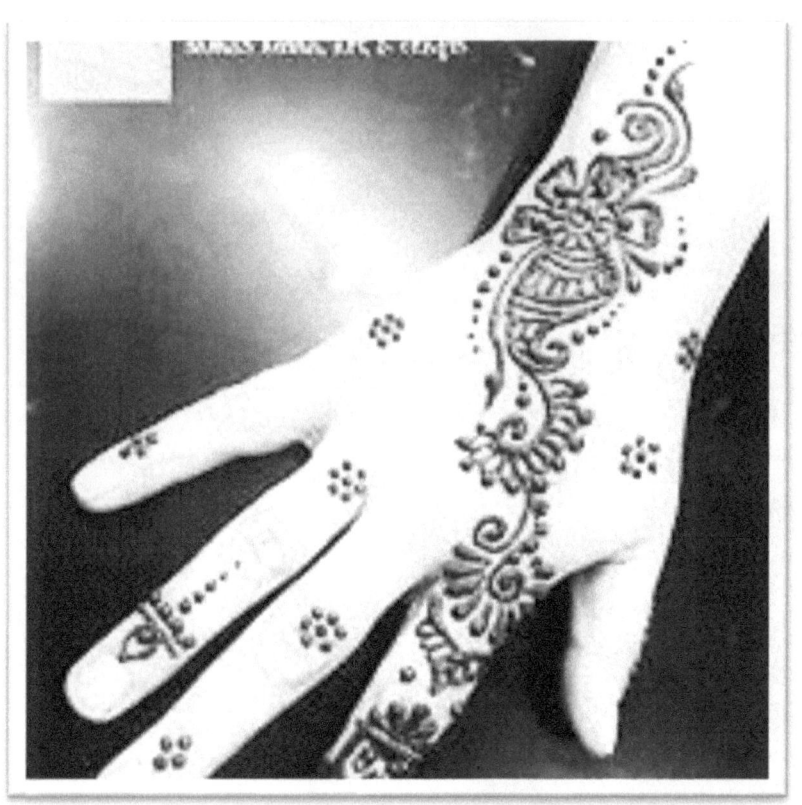

CUTENESS

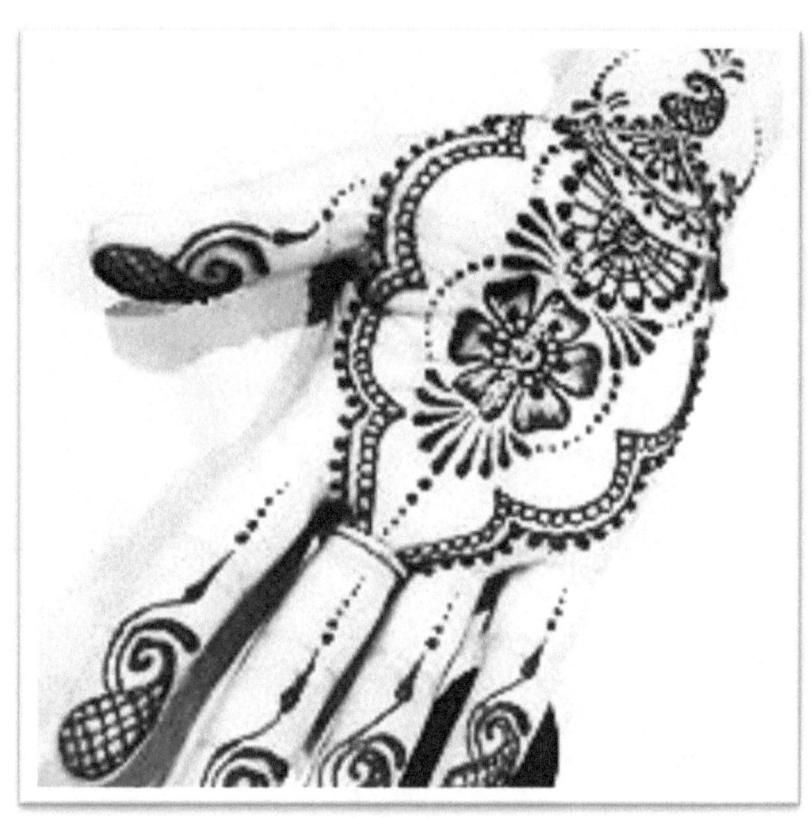

Brilliance

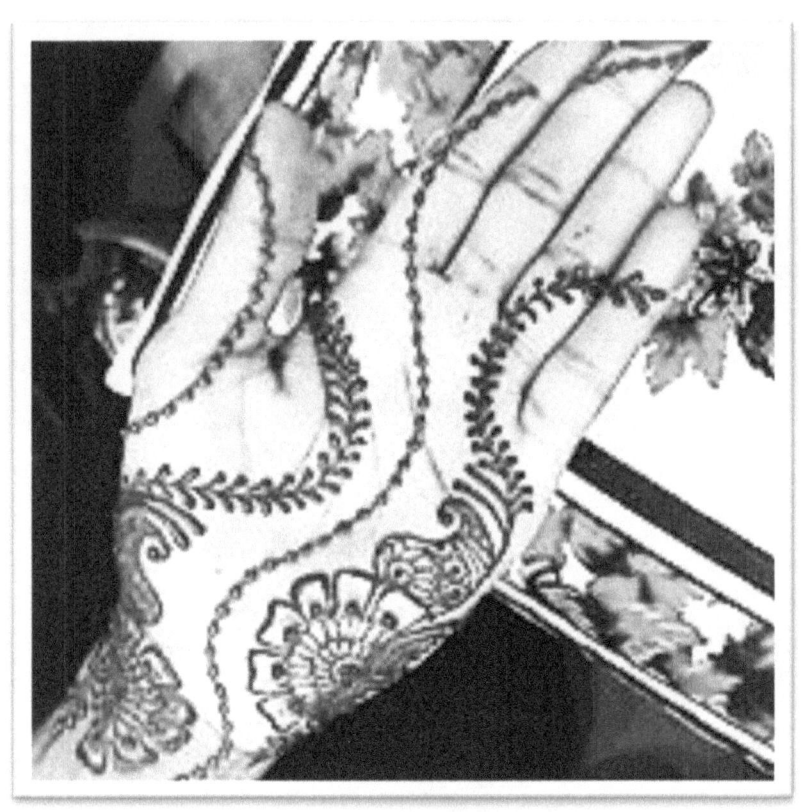

Splendor

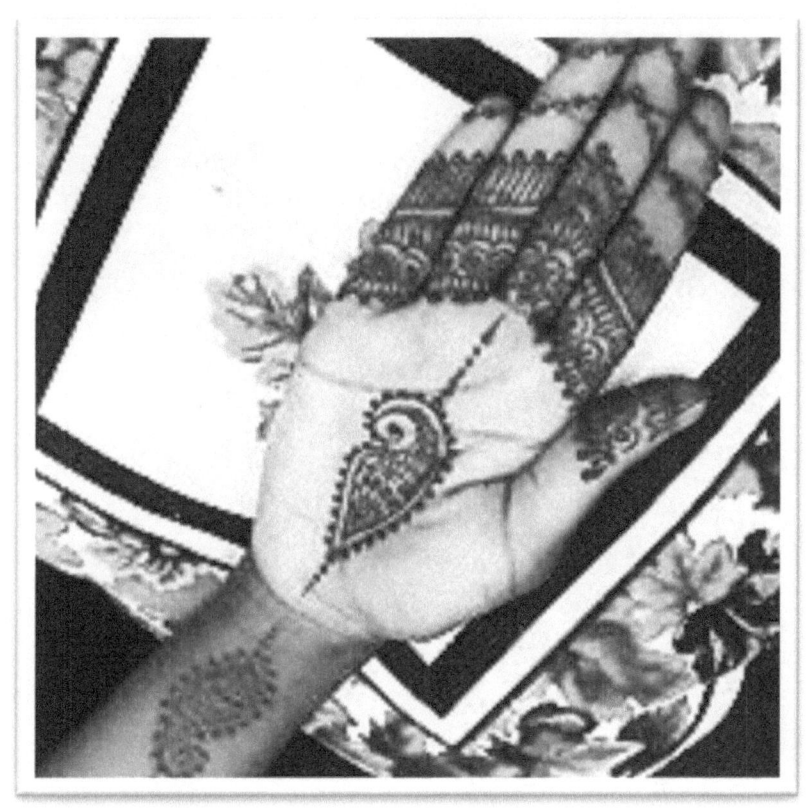

EXCELLENCE

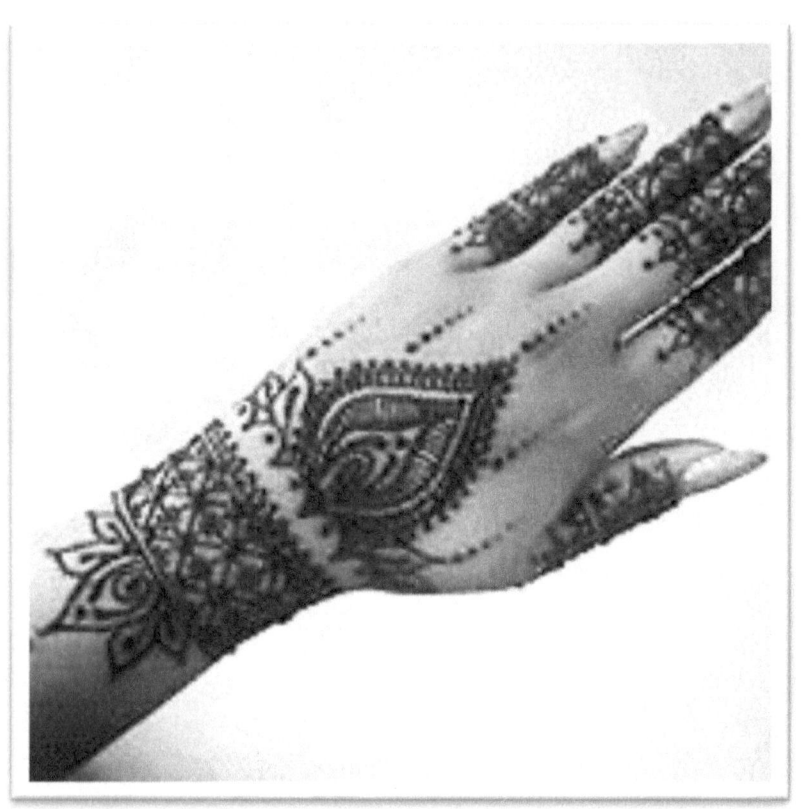

Elegance

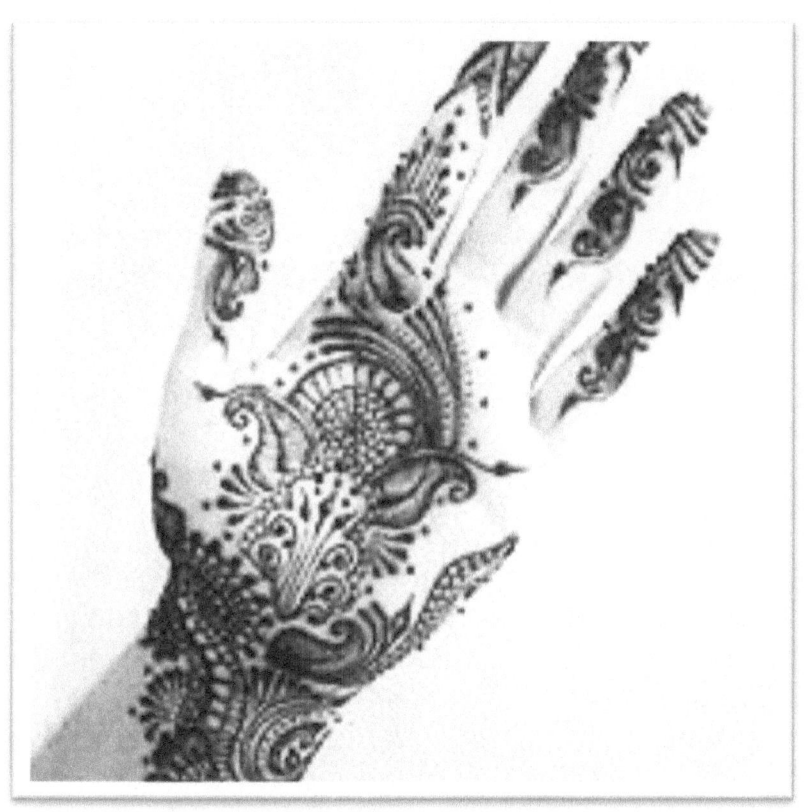

Exuberance

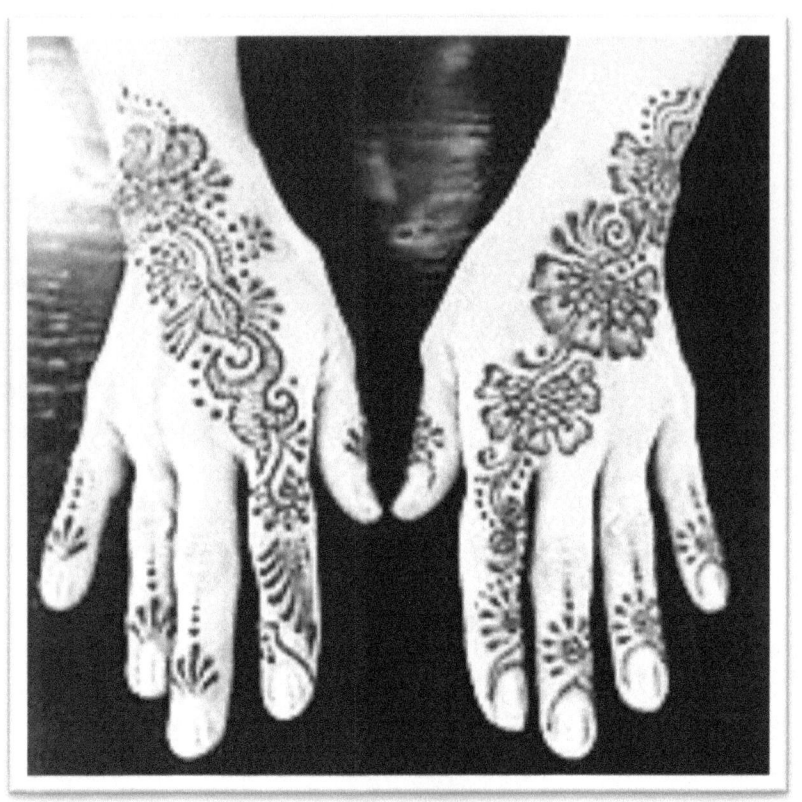

Together

This book is dedicated to my wonderful mother who first taught me all about henna when I was just a young girl and inspired me to learn how to do henna for others.

I love you mummy!